Summary:

The First 90 Days

By: Michael Watkins

Proudly Brought to you by:

Legal & Disclaimer

information provided by this guide. This disclaimer applies to any damages or injury caused by the use and application, whether directly or indirectly, of any advice or information presented, whether for breach of contract, tort, negligence, personal injury, criminal intent, or under any other cause of action.

You agree to accept all risks of using the information presented in this book. You need to consult a professional medical practitioner to ensure you are both able and healthy enough to participate in this program.

Table of Contents

The Book at a Glance

Managers at every level of any organization often find themselves susceptible and exposed to the vagaries of the position because most often. They do not possess the experience and the knowledge of the job content and the unseen challenges that they will face as they try to succeed in their new position or company.

The author believes that the first 90 days in a new leadership position is critical because not being able to create any momentum as a leader will practically guarantee an uphill and challenging adventure for the rest of a new leader's tenure.

The word, "roadmap" is most often used to describe Michael Watkin's book, and rightfully so, because it is an invaluable guide for those who find themselves "stranded."

In the road to restoring organizational order. That the book is already in its 10th edition shows how popular and widely-read this roadmap is. The book can also be seen as a guidebook or workbook, where each following chapter helps the new leader build upon skills and knowledge obtained from the previous section.

Each chapter in *The First 90 Days,* which has been translated into over 25 languages, begins with a real-life situation which helps us to get familiar and comfortable with the concepts of that particular chapter.

In Chapter 1, the author describes how we need to realize our new role in the organization, to "leave our past behind," and start trailblazing a new one. Part of this crucial process is to take stock of our abilities and limitations to prepare us for this big leap better.

Chapter 2, shows us how to learn to make the proper investment in learning about our new position. There is so much new knowledge to master and absorb, so we learn where to focus our energies on the information most crucial to our new role.

In Chapter 3. We learn to correctly match the strategy to our situation which begins with diagnosing the business situation carefully. Only after we have diagnosed the condition can you act wisely about the challenges of your new job and the opportunities and resources available to us.

Chapter 4 mostly describes how a new leader deals with a new boss or bosses. The "negotiation" between and new leader and the boss is about setting expectations for the new role and creating milestones and deliverables for this new relationship.

Chapter 5 points out the importance of getting off to a fast start in implementing changes, improving the performance of the organization, and creating a "new" compelling vision. All this should be accomplished while building personal credibility and a positive reputation. It also identifies pitfalls and traps to avoid in performance during the first 90 days.

Chapter 6 describes how new leaders should be able to start streamlining the organization by their vision. New leaders should become so-called, "organizational architects" who can align the organization's culture, its team's skills, the systems, structure, and strategy with their own.

Chapter 7 describes how new leaders should deal with the teams that they inherit, including how they can weave in organizational and structural changes with the minimum of stress and disruption. New leaders must also manage the tension between long-term goals and short-term objectives since they will be new agents of a change who will be expected to introduce and implement new team processes.

In Chapter 8, the author warns about the trap that makes news leaders believe that their position and authority are enough. There are crucial alliances that new leaders must forge, and it is critical that they be able to identify these. New leaders must map their networks of influence, and determine where they need to focus.

Chapter 9 leverages on the discoveries and revelations that new managers learn in Chapter 1. After chapters 4 through 8 describe detailed steps in dealing with others in the organization, this section dwells on personal disciplines, and how to create and enforce them. Watkins also shows how to set up an advising and counseling function within the organization to provide a feedback network for new leaders.

Finally, Chapter10 provides a way for new leaders to not only impose their new look on the organization, but to accelerate the transition of the organization to a common framework that details their unique vision, style, and objectives. The new leaders should then work to make the organization institutionalize these.

Dr. Michael Watkins is one of the world's top experts on accelerating transitions in organizations. He has taught at the INSEAD in France, and at the Harvard Business School, the Kennedy School of Government at Harvard University, and is currently Professor of Leadership and Organizational Change at the International Institute for Management Development in Switzerland. He is also a regular contributor to the Harvard Business Review and is a regular speaker on the management lecture circuit.

Aside from *The First 90 Days,* he also wrote: *Critical Success Strategies for New Leaders,* and *Your Next Move: The Leader's Guide to Successfully Navigating Major Career Transitions.* He consults on organizational transitions through his company, Genesis Advisers, which he founded with Shawna Stack, another business transitions expert.

Dr. Watkins is a Canadian citizen and has a Ph.D. in Decision Sciences from Harvard University. He received an electrical engineering undergraduate degree from the University of Waterloo in Ontario, Canada, and also attended the University of Western Ontario, where he studied law and business.

FREE BONUSES

P.S. Is it okay if we overdeliver?

Here at Readtrepreneur Publishing, we believe in overdelivering way beyond our reader's expectations. Is it okay if we overdeliver?

Here's the deal, we're going to give you an extremely condensed PDF summary of the book which you've just read and much more…

What's the catch? We need to trust you… You see, we want to overdeliver and in order for us to do that, we've to trust our reader to keep this bonus a secret to themselves? Why? Because we don't want people to be getting our exclusive PDF summaries even without buying our books itself. Unethical, right?

Ok. Are you ready?

Firstly, remember that your book is code: "**READ96**".

Next, visit this link: http://bit.ly/exclusivepdfs

Everything else will be self explanatory after you've visited: http://bit.ly/exclusivepdfs.

We hope you'll enjoy our free bonuses as much as we enjoyed preparing it for you!

Introduction

The nature of transitioning to higher levels of management has changed dramatically over the past few years. Long gone are the days where people stayed in one company for their entire working lives, go up the ranks a few times, with very few making it to the top positions. Today, people not only move up much more quickly within organizations, but there are more and more managers and executives jumping ship to other organizations.

Leaders on the average, "transition" 13.5 times over their working lives, including promotions and transfers, meaning people move on the average, every 1.3 years. This makes transitioning a key event in any manager or executive's life, and it is important that these are handled with as much competence as possible.

There's good news and bad news when competent people get promoted or hired for positions of leadership whether the move is within their organizations, or to new ones. On the good side, transitions to leadership levels allow newly minted leaders to start anew and infuse much needed "fresh blood" to their new position or company. On the other hand, transitions can make new leaders extremely vulnerable, because they are thrown in an environment where there is rarely a detailed understanding of their new roles, and more critically, there is a lack of established working relationships.

Making the situation worse is that new leaders are placed under extreme scrutiny, as people in the organization are eager to have a leader represent them, and find out what they are made of. Initial opinions are important at this stage, because views of their competence and effectiveness are very difficult to change, once they are formed.

The goal of every new leader is to get to the "break-even" point of their position as quickly as possible. This break-even point is defined as that point early in a new position where new leaders have consumed as much from the organization, as they have contributed to it. New leaders are net "users" of value early in their tenures as they take tentative steps learning the ropes to figure out what the position is all about, before they start to take action, and create value in their new positions. The book is all about trying to shorten this path to the break-even and making that route as painless and efficient as possible.

There is some empirical evidence about the time it takes to get to this break-even point. Experts believe that getting to the break-even point takes about six months or 180 days. However, if the transition is done properly, it can take half that time or 90 days. However, even before taking on the first 90 days, there are general missteps that new leaders have to avoid:

1. Sticking with what you know – New leaders must realize that they are not improved models of their former position, but they are NEW models of a different mold.;

2. Needing to take action right away – Being too eager to do something positive right away, without assessing the possible consequences;

3. Setting unrealistic expectations – Goals need to be set in alignment with others and setting achievable goals;

4. Attempting to do too much – In a rush to establish their bonafides, new leaders can launch themselves in all directions, investing much quantity of work, with quality as a secondary consideration. This will confuse people, and resources are in danger of being misapplied;

5. Coming in with "the" answer –New leaders come up with their "aha!" moments and arrive at conclusions prematurely possibly without considering alternatives that could even be better;

6. Engaging in the wrong type of learning – New leaders may feel that they quickly need to get up to speed on the technical knowledge required on the job, and ignoring the cultural and values perspectives which are just as important. They may be spending too much time learning "what," instead of knowing "how."; and

7. Neglecting horizontal relationships – New leaders may start getting overly concerned with the boss, and not spend enough time with peers and subordinates, who are usually closer to the frontlines and have more unfiltered information.

The preceding missteps can lead to a "vicious" cycle of transitions that include inadequate learning, ineffective relationship building, lack of supportive alliances, bad decisions, lost credibility, and resistance from all levels. They have to get into a good cycle of the correct activities to achieve success.

A new leader's overriding objective is to generate momentum by doing the right steps towards a VIRTUOUS CYCLE, instead of a vicious one. This is a cycle of getting "early wins," obtaining supportive alliances, earning increasing credibility, making good decisions, proceeding with an informed vision and strategy, focusing their learning, and most importantly, building effective relationships. While a leader is just one, a single person, this individual's success depends on the

5

ability to harness the energy of others in the organization and drive the organization forward.

There is a system to avoid transition failures which may happen because new leaders lack the flexibility and skill to adapt to the demands of their new situation, a situation which may be misunderstood in the first place. The system to deal with this consists of the following steps, which are described in a chapter devoted to each of them:

1. Prepare yourself,

2. Accelerate your learning,

3. Match your strategy to the situation,

4. Secure early wins,

5. Negotiate success,

6. Achieve alignment,

7. Create coalitions,

8. Keep your balance, and

9. Accelerate everyone.

Chapter 1. Prepare Yourself

<u>Getting Promoted</u>

In older editions of the book, this chapter was titled. "Promote yourself," and self-promotion continues to be an important aspect of this all-important first chapter. "Promoting yourself" does not mean engaging in some manner of grandstanding, self-aggrandizement public type of behavior. Self-promotion means setting yourself up mentally to transition into your new role by leaving your past and getting a running start on your duties by putting in the time and effort to learn all you can about your new job.

As you move up, you will realize that it takes a lot more effort to do this, as your responsibilities grow. You can get promoted by your superiors to a new position, but you need to promote yourself internally by working hard to learn more about your new job and yourself.

The hardest part of transitioning to a new leadership role is breaking away mentally from a previous job or position. For example, a CFO promoted to CEO may think that his CFO skills of being detail-oriented can work in his CEO role, which requires being able to take a 50,000-foot view of things. A newly promoted leader must make a "mental break" from the old job, and immediately begin preparing for the new position. This is a widespread mistake which can and should be avoided. The following challenges immediately present themselves to new leaders:

1. Balancing depth and breadth – A higher position means a wider scope of responsibilities. New leaders must balance this breadth of scope with how much depth of detail they need to go into;

2. Rethinking what needs to be delegated – Delegation starts with building a competent core of people who will work for new leaders. The next step is to have a feedback mechanism and metrics to measure the performance of those who are delegated work. Finally, the number and expertise of people change dramatically

as leaders climb up the organizational ladder. CEOs for example, will delegate to a much smaller number of people, but this group will have much stronger skills and influence in the organization;

3. Influence differently – As leaders get increasingly higher responsibilities, decision making is not only less about authority and more about influence, but it also involves a lot more politics. This is inevitable because issues are more ambiguous and complex. Data and information are less relied upon to come up with the right answers. Decisions at higher levels are more about who trusts whom and by the expert judgments of other people. Also, new leaders deal with new players who are more skilled, and have bigger ego; so new leaders have to form key alliances and develop different approaches to coming up with decisions;

4. Communicate more formally – Information that new leaders receive change as their responsibilities increase. New leaders are further removed from the frontlines than before, so information is more filtered. To get better information and communicate better, new leaders

must establish ways to make sure that communications allow for the right amount and type of information to travel to and from them; and

5. Exhibit the right presence - the Public image is more important for new leaders. Questions asked are, "What kind of personal leadership attributes do they have?", "How do they act?" and, "What is their leadership brand?". New leaders are more visible, and they need to deal with this higher profile.

OVERBOARDING INTO A NEW COMPANY

When new leaders come "on board" to a higher management level, especially in a new company, there are four pillars of overboarding that they need to remember so that the transition is more effective and fluid:

1. Business Orientation – In plain terms, new leaders must understand the nature of the business: understanding talent procurement and management, performance evaluation systems, planning systems, and

10

the operating models and platforms that the organizations run on;

2. Stakeholder Connection – New leaders need to identify and develop key working relationships as soon as possible for a smoother transition;

3. Expectations Alignment – It is essential for new leaders to adjust and align their pre-conceived expectations to the new organization. However, new leaders must manage and align the expectations of others, especially their bosses; and

4. Cultural Adaptation – The culture of an organization is a set of predictable and consistent patterns that people follow to act, think, communicate, and follow, based on their values and assumptions.

PREPARING YOURSELF

New leaders should have the following "checklists" and activities as they begin the transition process:

1. Business orientation checklist - As early as possible, new leaders should obtain and review information

available to the public such as investors. These will include prospectuses, financial statements, annual reports, and similar material.

New leaders should also talk to their boss to help them identify and get introduced you to the pivotal people that they should connect with. The new leaders should also get together with stakeholders from all levels in the organization before they even commence their project. These should include not only vertical relationships such as direct reports and bosses but also those in lateral relationships, such as peers. They should have a tightly controlled calendar that includes meetings with stakeholders as early in the process as possible.

2. Expectations alignment checklist – New leaders should understand and be engaged in business planning as well as performance management. Regardless of how well they believe they know what they need to do, they should still schedule a conversation with the boss regarding expectations. Ideally, this should be done in the first few days. They need to have clear conversations

regarding working styles with the bosses as well as how direct reports would be carried out as early as possible.

3. Cultural adaptation checklist - New leaders should learn about the culture and politics of the organization. This is done by observation, and by conversations with people who have long tenures, and have "seen everything."

4. Establish a clear breakpoint -It is important for new leaders to tell themselves that they have truly "moved on" from their previous positions. This is when new leaders will accept that their new assignments are not merely extensions of their previous responsibilities.

5. Assess vulnerabilities and strengths – New leaders should make a comprehensive review of their skills vis-à-vis the future job, and determine what forces and advantages they can bring to the job. They should also make a frank assessment of any deficiencies in experience and skill so that they can be ready for any consequences related to these.

6. Relearn how to learn – New leaders not only need to learn new things, they should adjust their mindset to focus on the different way they need to learn – concentrate on the bigger picture, and being more strategy- instead of process-focused.

7. Rework their network – A changing environment means that new relationships and types of relationships need to be established and cultivated. New leaders should also watch out for people who want to hold you back and get help from as many reliable people in their network as they can.

Chapter 2. Accelerate Your Learning

OVERCOMING LEARNING ROADBLOCKS

The most significant roadblock is the failure to PLAN TO LEARN. What this means is that some new leaders do not realize that learning about their new roles and the needs of the new organization requires a planned, disciplined approach. They need to know more about the history of the organization, its people, and its systems using a structured method of learning.

In the introduction, we talked about the so-called "action imperative," where new leaders want to jump in and accomplish tasks right away almost compulsively. There has to be a proper balance between "being" (reflecting and observing) and "doing" (getting things done). There are just too many NEW things to learn about a new role/organization to allow the "doing" to be an overwhelming priority.

This applies even when new leaders are brought in to engineer turnarounds or rehabilitation. While they are brought in to import their ways of doing things, there are still cultural differences that are unique to the new organization, and the approach to completing the usual tasks still require some customization.

MANAGING LEARNING AS AN INVESTMENT PROCESS

The critical term in the learning process is an "ACTIONABLE INSIGHT." This refers to a piece of knowledge or observation that new leaders can act upon to enable them to reach their break-even point faster as they make better decisions. For example, new leaders may find out that there is a management tendency to underinvest in worthwhile projects. While this is insight, it also offers the opportunity for a new leader to propose action to at least know why this behavior takes place. Determining actionable insights is crucial in moving the transition forward.

New leaders will facilitate their journey to the breakeven point if they can extract the maximum number of quality insights in the shortest time possible.

DEFINING YOUR LEARNING AGENDA

A learning agenda always starts with questions to start to develop and identify actionable insights. These questions need to be written down, and can be classified into one of three categories:

1. Questions about the past – These questions are about actual results and performance, determining the causes of these findings, and what benchmarks were used to define these measurements. Questions also need to be asked as to how performance issues were addressed, and who was responsible for addressing them;

2. Questions about the present – These questions ask what the mission and vision of the organization are, whether these are being followed, and who is responsible for making sure these are followed. Questions also need to be asked about the people as to capability, influence, and trustworthiness. The processes of the organization also need to be understood, together with identifying what possible "land mines" are lurking which could sabotage not only the new leaders' agenda but the organization's well-being; and

3. Questions about the future – The questions to be asked include identifying opportunities and challenges, identifying possible changes in processes and manpower, identifying barriers and resources available, and determining if any changes to culture need to be made, and which culture elements are worth preserving.

Over time, the learning agenda morphs from question-asking to hypotheses-forming as new leaders begin to get answers, and ideas about their new roles and organization begin to crystallize. In answering these questions, new leaders should identify where they can score the "early wins," such as improving processes, tightening the vision, and streamlining human resources

IDENTIFYING THE BEST SOURCES OF INSIGHT

Hard data such as employee surveys, functional plans, industry reports, press accounts, operating reports, and financial statements are easily available. However, you will also need so-called "soft" information, which is not readily available from public sources. This includes information about the organization's technical capabilities, strategy, politics, and probably the hardest to obtain, yet most important to consider: culture.

The most effective way to obtain this information is to talk to people. Some of these people will come from within the company:

1. Operations and frontline R&D – They develop and manufacture products or deliver the services of the organization. They provide information on processes and how the organization relates to outside parties such as the community and competitors;

2. Procurement and sales – These people deal with customers, their representatives, vendors, and suppliers. They can provide current information about market trends on both the sales and purchasing aspects;

3. Staff – Key people in human resources, finance, and the legal department, can provide useful if specialized, perspectives on how the organization works;

4. Integrators – These people coordinate interaction between different organizational functions, and include

19

key people such as product managers, plant managers, and project managers;

5. Natural "historians" - Those who have been with the organization for a long time have seen it gone through various trials, and can provide valuable insight on the roots of its politics and culture;

In the course of conversations with the above people, new leaders can extract clues about organizational politics, capabilities, culture, and where internal conflicts occur.

People outside the company are also important:

1. Customers.

2. Suppliers.

3. Distributors.

4. Outside Analysts – Consultants hired by the organization as well as outside observers can provide an objective view

Adopting Structured Learning Methods

The most important part of the learning process will require new leaders to ask the same questions to everybody, especially the direct reports. Uniform questions will help weed out biases. The questions are:

1. If you were me, what would you focus on?

2. To exploit the potential of unexploited opportunities, what events would need to ensure in the organization?

3. What are the most promising unexploited opportunities for growth?

4. Why is the organization facing (or going to face) these challenges?

5. What are the biggest challenges the organization is facing or will face?

New leaders can also use proven analytical techniques to help them in the learning process, such as S (Strengths), W (Weaknesses), O (Opportunities), T (Threats) analysis.

Creating a Learning Plan

The learning plan for new leaders should tightly follow the 90-day timetable as follows:

1. Before entry – Perform analysis of operations, processes, and reports of external observers and analysts. Put together a list of questions for direct reports to continue the analysis. Meet with the boss to discuss preliminary plans;

2. Soon after entry – Meet with direct reports one-on-one and provide them with a list of questions for further probing; and

3. Before the end of the first month – Gather the team and assess the answers to the questions, come up hypotheses on various aspects, analyze a few processes, meet with the boss to discuss findings.

Chapter 3. Match Strategy to Situation

For new leaders to succeed, they must above all, possess full awareness of the situation and a clear understanding of what needs to be done, and the knowledge that comes with being able to execute.

New leaders must ask two questions at the outset:

1. What kind of change am I being asked to bring?

2. What kind of a change leader am I?

THE STARS MODEL

This model answers the first question and throws out the "one size fits all approach to a problem. The acronym "S.T.A.R.S." stands for the five different change situations that new leaders can face:

1. (**S**)tartup – the New leader has to put get a new business off the ground by assembling the requisite funding, technologies, and people. This allows new leaders to have a major, if not the main role, in setting

the agenda, and putting together the business architecture, its processes, and relationships;

2. (**T**)urnaround - In this situation, new leaders are tasked to "rehabilitate" an organization that finds itself in deep trouble, and needs stewardship to get it back on the right course. This type of change management demands decisive, quick action and is the classic "burning platform."

3. (**A**)ccelerated Growth – In this situation, an organization has already started to hit its stride, and the challenge is how to scale up, by instituting new systems, processes, and structures to quickly grow an organization's business, or in the case of divisions, its relationships, products, or projects. Because the organization or project needs to be expanded, new leaders will likely need to onboard and hire a lot of new people from the outside.

These three change situations, (**S**)tartup, (T)urnaround, and (**A**)ccelerated. Growth does not provide the new leaders with the much-existing infrastructure to work with and will involve much work involving resource-intensive construction work.

4. (**R**)ealignment – Most organizations, even successful ones, can drift towards trouble, and the stewardship of a new leader will be needed to revitalize it before it careens into something much more serious. The storm has not yet hit, but the dark clouds are gathering on the horizon.

5. (**S**)ustained Success – In this situation, new leaders are given the burden to preserve an organization's vitality by bringing it to the next level. Many organizations in today's technology-focused environment either move on and move up or die. Just as sharks die if they stay still, so will some organizations. In this situation, new leaders must understand what brought the organization to this (successful) point and must try to replicate the success in bringing the organization to new heights.

All have different approaches and strategies. Some are perceived to be more difficult, and prospective leaders prefer to be involved in certain situations more than others:

A survey of managers revealed which situations they found most challenging (the first number) and the most preferred they would like to find themselves in.

Start-up (13.5%)47.1%

Turnaround (21.9%)16.7%

Accelerated growth (11.6%) 16.1%

Realignment (30.3%) 12.7%

Sustaining success (22.6%) 7.4%

The STARS model helps new leaders stay away from the "one-best-way" thinking, and forces them to diagnose the situation to develop the right strategy.

Diagnosing the STARS Portfolio

In practice, the higher up the organization a new leader is, the easier it is to pigeonhole an organization into one of the five STARS categories. However, it is common that when they drill down to analyze an enterprise-wide situation, a particular division, product, or project may be a different change situation than the overall organization.

Whatever STARS category an organization is in, a new leader must consider the following factors in analyzing their approach to lead the organization:

1. Organize to learn,

2. Define strategic intent,

3. Establish A-item priorities,

4. Build a leadership team,

5. Secure early wins,

6. Create supporting alliances,

LEADING CHANGE

Managing Yourself – What kind of leader is required

In tackling any of the five change situations, new leaders must have to figure out if they are reflexively a "steward" or a "hero." Heroes are usually sought after by people in turnaround situations because they are hungry for direction, vision, and hope. They are seen as relentless, and ego-driven; and with a sword in hand, they charge against the enemy.

On the other hand, new leaders in charge of realignments are seen almost as servant leaders, as stewards of a ship that need some guidance. New leaders of this endeavor are seen types not expected to charge the enemy, but are more diplomatic, signaling the need to build consensus even as they fight to institute changes.

In a situation where sub-leaders are needed, some projects and conditions may require a precise mix of stewards and heroes. It is a team game, and the team in any organization needs both.

REWARDING SUCCESS

There is no one-size-fits-all approach to performance evaluations. Evaluation and rewards must be done differently depending on what STARS situation is applicable. It is easier to evaluate the performance of start-ups and turnarounds because evaluators usually have actual outcomes that can be measured relative to a predetermined baseline which is often quantifiable in money or quantity terms.

It can be much different in sustaining success and realignment situations, however. Sometimes, success is measured in nothing happening, as in the case of a crisis being averted. Success may also be measured by sustaining a loss that is much smaller than initially feared or expected. It takes a lot more work to measure success in these situations and requires a much more in-depth knowledge of the issues facing the organization before and after the situation be addressed or rectified.

Chapter 4. Negotiate Success

The importance of the boss cannot be underestimated, because success needs to be negotiated, and the relationship between new leaders and the boss is one of, it not the most critical connections. The boss will have, more than any person, the most significant impact on how fast new leaders reach their break-even point. This relationship is of extreme importance because of the following:

1. The boss controls access to the resources that a new leader needs;

2. The boss interprets the actions of new leaders for other key players; and

3. The boss sets the benchmarks for achievement or success.

The "boss" can be a single person, a committee, a board of directors, or any group of people that has the authority to evaluate the success of a new leader.

<u>Focusing on the Fundamentals</u>

There are things that new leaders have to remember NOT to do about their bosses:

1. Don't stay away – New leaders should always show up when the boss says so;

2. Don't only go the boss when there are problems;

3. Don't surprise the boss – Bosses hate it when they are presented an issue that should have been discussed as it was developing, and not only when it has happened;

4. Don't run down a checklist – New leaders cannot expect their bosses to sit there and listen and respond to a series of numbing issues that may or may not be of interest or criticality to the boss;

5. Don't expect the boss to change – Rather, it is the attitude of new leaders towards a boss's personality or management style. It is often dangerous and fatal to try to change the attitudes of others, instead of changing ours first.

On the other hand, the following are "DO's" for new

leaders, when it comes to their bosses:

1. Assume ALL the responsibility to ensure that the relationship succeeds,

2. Negotiate timelines for action planning and diagnosis,

3. Clarify expectations early and often,

4. Obtain credibility from the people whose input the boss respects, and

5. Aim for early wins in areas that are important to the boss.

Planning for Five Conversations

These are five specific conversations that need to be done with a new leader's new boss as early as possible in the first 90 days. These are all transition-related, and it does not necessarily need to be dealt with in five separate conversations or meetings, but can be intertwined threads in a single meeting, or in a series of dialogues.

1 Situational diagnosis – The new leader and the boss agrees on the nature of the STARS portfolio that the new leader has inherited. Can the situation be pigeonholed in one STARS category, or is it a situation of combined change elements? The discussion will include how the organization got to that point, and what factors are making the situation the challenge that it is. Often, the boss' diagnosis will differ from the new leader's, and this is the time to clear the air;

2. Expectations of the new leader – This is where the boss lays out what is expected of the new leader in the short- and medium- term. What will be the definition of success? How will results and performance be measured? Unrealistic performance standards will need to be addressed in this conversation;

3. The resource conversation – This will be a negotiation on how much of critical resources will be allocated to the new leader. The new leaders will provide a baseline of what resources will ensure their success. These "resources" need not be necessarily material or financial in nature, but can be in the form of the boss providing his weight and influence in

convincing the rest of the organization on the criticality of the new leaders' participation and involvement;

4. The style conversation – This will clarify the manner and method as to how the new leaders will communicate with their boss on a continuing basis. Most often, the physical locations will be different, so an agreement must be reached on the methodology and timing of meetings, providing periodic updates, and the raising of questions. Also, will the communications be face to face? Electronic? Telephonic? Also, what kind of decisions will the boss be wanted to be consulted on? It is also a time to determine how different styles can be compromised on.

5. The personal development conversation – What is in it for the new leaders? As they approach completion, and after the completion, what awaits the leader as far as career and personal development goals?

While 90% of the chapter deals with the boss, the new leaders should also have these five conversations with their direct reports to ensure that a smooth transition ensues involving all levels of the organization.

Chapter 5. Secure Early Wins

New leaders should work hard in the early days in their new positions to make a difference by being efficient, efficient, knowledgeable while projecting an aura of command and self-assurance. Doing things right and on time (hopefully before deadlines), and being effective and efficient in their new roles are "wins" that will help them build personal credibility and help them gain momentum.

Within the first 90 days, new leaders should want your subordinates, peers, and bosses to feel that something good is happening underfoot, that a new wave of changes is happening which will benefit the group or the organization. Properly executed, new leaders can create value in their new role and enable them to achieve the break-even level more quickly.

<u>Making Waves</u>

There are four primary "waves" that a new leader will be involved in. The intensity of change is very low at the beginning but begins to increase by the end of the first 90 ninety days, which is the first wave. The intensity peaks in the reshaping wave, when the changes are first instituted, and the organization feels the effects of the change.

1. Transition Wave (0 to 3 months- The First Ninety Days – While much learning goes in in this wave, the primary goal is to get some early wins, so that new leaders build credibility, forge strong relationships with key personnel, and harvest "low-hanging fruit," which are apparent fixes that relate to short-term improvements to the organization. These early wins should as much as possible, allow the new leaders to introduce new behavioral patterns, and should be aligned with the agreed-upon goals, or those that were agreed upon by the boss and other key stakeholders. The focus should be on business priorities even if low-hanging fruit are snagged from time to time. The following three waves depend on the foundation that new leaders set for themselves in this transition phase.

2. Immersion Wave (3 to 6 months) – The new leaders are more entrenched in the organization in this wave, and they address structure, systems and processes, strategy, and skills to bring a new shape of the organization. This is where the early wins become important, as credibility becomes more important than ever.

3. Reshaping (6 months to 9 months) – The structural and organizational changes instituted by new leaders are put into place, and this is where most of the intense change happens, as new processes and structures are INSTALLED and implemented. This is where much resistance comes in, especially from those who are invested and entrenched in the old ways of doing things.

4. Consolidation (9 months to 18 months and beyond) – The changes instituted by the new leaders are in place, and the organization begins its day-to-day operations incorporating the changes. This is about the time that new leaders entrench themselves in their leadership positions, desire to move on to other challenges, or are asked by management to take on bigger challenges.

Each of the above waves should be comprised of learning, change design, support building, change implementation, and the observation of results. A key in each stream is to identify and address problematic behavior patterns which are lack of:

1. Focus,

2. Discipline,

3. Innovation,

4. Teamwork, and

5. The sense of Urgency.

ADOPTING BASIC PRINCIPLES

To ensure a smooth transition, new leaders must adopt the following principles while securing early wins:

1. Focus on a few promising opportunities – New leaders cannot be all things to all people. Given that they only have a limited time to make an impact, they should not take on too much, or face disastrous consequences. They should only take on what can yield

achievable results in the short period, given the other constraints discussed below. They should look for enough promising areas without diffusing their efforts.

2. Get wins that matter to the boss – In Chapter 4, we discussed the importance of the boss in the transition process. Early wins need to be those that energize not only direct reports, but primarily, the boss. The bosses' opinions are crucial because what they say will help build credibility, and encourage the bosses to allocate more resources.

3. Get wins in the right ways – The higher up the ladder a new leader goes, the more political things become, and culture becomes a factor. New leaders who gain impressive results in ways that can be viewed as inconsistent with the organization's culture, or through actions that are seen as underhanded and manipulative, are setting themselves up for disaster. Early wins done by acceptable behavior is a double win because it builds up credibility and trust.

4. Take your STARS portfolio into account - What constitutes an early win differs dramatically from one

STARS business situation to another. Simply getting people to talk about the organization and its challenges can be a big accomplishment in a realignment, but it is a waste of time in a turnaround. So new leaders need to think hard about what will build momentum best in each part of their portfolio. Will it be a demonstrated willingness to listen and learn? Will it be rapid, decisive calls on pressing business issues?

5. Adjust to the culture. In some organizations, a win must be a visible and momentous individual accomplishment. However, in others, the individual pursuit of glory is viewed as grandstanding and harmful for teamwork, even if it does produce good results. In team-oriented organizations, early wins could come in the form of leading a team in the development of a new product idea or being viewed as a solid contributor and team player in a broader initiative. New leaders should ensure that they understand what is and is not viewed as a win, especially if you are onboarding into the organization.

IDENTIFY THE EARLY WINS

New leaders will need to build personal credibility in roughly the first 30 days, and then decide which projects they will launch to achieve early performance improvements beyond that. These new initiatives can be determined only if the early wins are properly identified and analyzed. Future wins after the first 90 days can then be patterned after these first wins.

Chapter 6. Achieve Alignment

New leaders are supposed to be "organizational architects, where they are expected to align the key elements of the organization: Skill base, core processes, structure, and strategic direction. Popularity and charisma alone will not accomplish much if the organization is out of alignment. Apart from doing the right things, there are also wrong things to avoid:

<u>Avoid Common Traps</u>

1. Making changes for change's sake – New leaders can be tempted to score those early wins just to have the win recorded for posterity, even if the changes do not have net value to the organization. This is a waste of valuable resources.

2. Not adjusting for the STARS situation – Once again, there is no one size fits all approach to a change situation. A proper understanding of circumstances is needed to determine the approach to the change situation.

3.. Trying to restructure the way out of more profound problems – Changing the organization's structure is a tempting, high level, knee-jerk solution for a new leader. It is easy to move boxes around on a chart, when the problem may be in processes, skill bases, and culture.

4. Creating structures that are too complex - New leaders can become overly analytical and technical when figuring out reporting relationships and accountability. Lines of responsibility can be made clear even with simple structures.

5. Overestimating the organization's capacity to absorb change -   Many new leaders are eager to get the ball rolling, but they must be sure that not everything and everyone moves at the same speed they do, and some changes need to be made incrementally, so as not to create too much havoc.

Designing Organizational Architecture

New leaders have to determine the structures of their units and organizations, and often, they do not have the experience to approach the problem in a more granular fashion. The best way to start analyzing and organizing changes is to start looking at the organization as an OPEN SYSTEM.

An open system starts with the assumption that all organizations are affected, and in turn affect, internal and external factors. That is, the organization is open to the interior environment comprised of culture, morale, and climate. It is also open to external players, such as the media, investors, customers, competitors, suppliers, distributors, and probably the most important, customers. The choices that new leaders make in the creation of their structure must make the situation responsive to the realities of the internal and external environments.

The four key elements of an organizational architecture will only work together correctly if they are aligned:

1. Strategic direction – The organization's stated strategy, and its mission and vision statement. This is the overriding element, and often the other three elements below need to work in concert with the overall strategy.

2.Structure – Not just comprised of an organizational chart, but also a description of how everyone is organized in units, how they coordinate their work, and how they are incentivized.

3. Core processes – The procedures and workflows that are utilized to add value to the processing of materials and information,

4. Skill bases - The competencies and skills of key groups of individuals.

Diagnosing Misalignments

In the first 90 days, new leaders must identify potential misalignments and then devise a strategy to correct them. The usual misalignments are as follows:

1.Misalignments between strategic direction and skill bases,

2. Misalignments between strategic direction and core processes,

3. Misalignments between structure and processes, and

4. Misalignments between structure and skills.

Getting the alignment started

Alignment is like going on a sailing trip. New leaders must be clear as to the proper destination (goals, mission, and vision) and route (strategy). Then they determine which sailing vessel is needed (structure), how it should be outfitted (processes), and the composition of the crew (skill base). Along the way, the new leaders need to watch for any dangerous, uncharted reefs that may sabotage the voyage.

The steps in aligning the organization are as follows:

1. Define strategic direction,

2. Review the supporting structure, processes, and skills,

3. Decide how and when the new strategic direction will be introduced,

4. Determine the proper sequencing of the three steps above. New leaders should consider the STARS model to determine this proper sequence, and

5. Close the loop.

46

Chapter 7. Build Your Team

One of the most, if not the most, important jobs for a new leader is to organize a high-performance team. New leaders cannot fulfill lofty objectives on their own since an organization is an organic structure made up of many people working together towards these goals. Poor personnel decisions during the first 90 days will come back to haunt the new leader and plague the organization for a long time. In building a team, new leaders must avoid the following common traps:

1, Criticize the previous leadership,

2. Keep the current team longer than necessary,

3. Not balancing stability and change,

4. Not working on team development and organizational alignment in parallel,

5. Not holding on to the right people,

6. Building the team before the key and core individuals are in place,

7. Premature adoption of implementation-making decisions, and

8. Trying to do everything themselves.

The phases of building the team are done in four phases: Assessing the current personnel, setting up (evolving) the team, aligning the team to the organization's objectives, and leading the team during actual operations.

ASSESSMENT

In the previous chapter, organizational alignment was discussed as crucial in the first 90 days. In putting a team together, the assessment phase addresses "what-is" as the existing personnel base is analyzed to determine the excellent skill base and organization.

New leaders will inherit staff with differing capabilities and records of performance. There will be the "A players," or exceptional staff, the "B players," or average staff, and the "C players," who have not lived up to standards. In the first month or so, this existing complement must be assessed to determine what their future roles, if any, will be in the organization.

The following need to be accomplished by the new leaders during the assessment phase:

1. Establish "cultural" criteria for evaluating EXISTING staff based on their current environment- Staff will be graded based on the following characteristics: Trustworthiness, focus, ability to get along with others, energy, and judgment. They should be scored on each of these characteristics, and ranked based on how they score;

2. Check assumptions after scoring – Determine what are the most important characteristics depending on the organization's current situation, and base personnel decisions based on how people rate in these characteristics;

3. Factor in functional expertise - Determine how everyone can contribute any specific talent or expertise in the new organization;

4. Factor in teamwork – This is teamwork not in the past tense (evaluated in 1.). This is teamwork that will be required in the new structure. This evaluation measures

how teams will work together under new operating guidelines and processes;

5. Factor in the STARS mix/situation - Different personalities will fit in different change situations; i.e., getting in the right mix of heroes and stewards;

6. Factor in the criticality of certain positions – How crucial is the staffing of a certain position? A "B" person may be needed for a highly critical function, while an "A" type person may be dispensable;

7. Plan to replace the people that fail in initial assessments; and

8. Conduct the meetings of the evaluation with existing staff – In these meetings, new leaders should have an interview template ready with the same questions asked of everyone. New leaders should ask questions that test the judgment of the personnel, while they look for verbal and non-verbal clues that are signs of people's consistency between thought and action, commitment, and honesty.

EVOLVING THE TEAM

After the assessment is completed, new leaders must begin forming their teams.

By the end of the first 30 days, new leaders should already be able to make assessments of what to do with the existing staff. These will be in the form of the following:

1. Retain the worker in the current position.

2. Retain a worker who needs development, and ensures that there are resources to help to do this.

3. Move a strong performer to another position where the person can make the most of personal qualities or skills.

4. Replace the person, although the situation is not urgent.

5. Replace the person immediately.

6. Place the person under observation, while leaders still need to make further observations.

51

ALIGNING THE TEAM

New leaders should use make sure that their assembled personnel understand how they can help achieve the organization's goals. The leaders will use both "push" and "pull" tools to motivate their people. Both tools will move the team into the alignment of the organization's goals and vision while bringing the team in line with proper motivation and direction.

Push tools are used to motivate people through the expectation of reward for productive work, fear, loyalty, and authority. Push tools include providing a vision statement, clear procedures and processes, an effective reporting system, and of course, incentives, including monetary and career-related ones.

Pull tools, on the other hand, are used to inspire people by providing an exciting and positive image of the future, and projecting a compelling "what could be" vision. New leaders should tap into inspirational sources, founded on such things as a contribution to society, and teamwork, and make organization personnel part of the "story."

LEADING THE TEAM

With the team assembled and aligned, the new leaders must now take the recurring organization day-to-day, and week-to-week basis. The new leaders determine what processes will be used to get the job done, recognizing that teams differ widely in how responsibilities are divided, conflict resolution, decision-making, and handling of meetings.

New leaders must do the following:

1. Assess existing processes – Determine participants' roles, figure out how meetings are to be conducted, determine the decision-making processes, as well as the leadership styles that are evident,

2. Target which processes need changing,

3. Change the participants in key decision-making meetings and processes,

4. Lead in the decision-making, and

5. Adjust for virtual teams when some members may be working directly.

Chapter 8. Create Alliances

The success of new leaders depends on the support of those outside their direct line of command. They need to assemble coalitions to ensure their success because the direct authority will never suffice to ensure success. New leaders must create informal bonds among colleagues, called "influence networks," that will help them get support for their goals and ideas. They need an influence strategy, to determine whom they will include in this coalition, which should include people who are most likely to support their agenda, and who can help them bring over "swing voters" on board. New leaders should undertake the following:

1. Define the influence objectives – New leaders need to ask, "Why do we need to influence people?" They will then need to have a clear understanding of what they are trying to achieve on a long-basis, and drill down to more detail, and find out whose support is critical, and how they can get these people on board. A good place to start is by figuring which of the early wins can be used

to gain the support of others, and where they have insufficient, or even, no authority. Early wins reflect the fulfillment of incremental steps towards the ultimate goals of the organization; and

2. Understand the influence landscape – New leaders must determine whom they need to get on board to help them support them in the early wins. They need to identify among everyone, who the key decision makers are, what they need these decision-makers to do, and when they are supposed to do it. New leaders need to create a list of who can help them, together with what these people need to do, and when.

After identifying this coalition, new leaders will also put a list together of people outside this coalition who can further support their agenda. These people can be broken down into the following:

a. Supporters - This will include new people who have yet been acculturated to the current operations, people who have been slowly and quietly working for changes, and most importantly, people who share the new leaders' vision of the future.

55

b. Persuadables - These are uncommitted, undecided, or indifferent about new leaders' initiatives, but may be convinced to provide support if it can be determined how they may be influenced.

c. Opponents - These people oppose new leaders' agenda because of any of, or a combination of, the following:

i. They are comfortable with the status quo and reject any change,

ii. Fear of looking incompetent,

iii. The new leader's changes are a threat to their core values,

iv. New leaders are threats to their power,

v. New leaders' agenda will have negative consequences for their allies.

<u>3</u>. Understand pivotal people – Within the organization, leaders will have to identify which people are crucial to the furtherance of the overall goals, as well as the sub-objectives not only because of their skill but also because of the credibility and personal influence they can exert on others in the organization.

4. Craft influence strategies – This step involves utilizing the pivotal people for the various functions and strategies critical to the achievement of objectives. This is combining steps (1) to (3) above to assemble the optimum alliances.

Chapter 9. Manage Yourself

New leaders' lives can be challenging. The life of a leader is always a balancing act, but never more so than during a transition phase. The ambiguity and uncertainty of daily life can be difficult. New leaders feel like they are on an island, still not having a support network, and not only know what they need to know but not knowing WHAT THEY DON'T KNOW. It not only affects the new leaders themselves but also their families, who have to live with the leaders in transition. Still, there are only 90 days for transition, and they will need to manage themselves, a transition challenge in itself. To accomplish this, they will need to perform the following steps:

1, Take Stock

Early on in the process, most preferably within the first month, new leaders should ask the following questions:

How Do You Feel So Far?

What Has Bothered You So Far?

What Has Gone Well or Poorly?

If there are any ill feelings towards their jobs, the new leaders must figure out what are the causes of any issues that bother them. These ill feelings can arise because of :

a. Undefended boundaries – New leaders need to establish boundaries on what they are willing, and not willing to do for the organization and its people. Doing too much or too little can be harmful to their credibility.

b. Brittleness – New leaders, especially those who have a high need for control, can find themselves defensive and rigid. They may make mistakes and refuse to accept responsibility, and also may feel that it is their way, and nothing else. This rigidity will be calamitous to new leaders' credibility and effectiveness.

c. Isolation – Failure to trust and not to establish the right connections in the first place may make new leaders unable to cooperate with others in the organization. They may discourage people to share important information critical to the organization. This lack of information will make them less efficient in the performance of their jobs.

d. Work avoidance - New leaders by choice, or even unconsciously, may elect to bury themselves in work or fool themselves into believing that the time is not right to come to a decision. This is what experts term as "avoidance" – hesitating to grab the bull by the horns that can result in problems not being addressed, making them even worse.

2, Understand the Three Pillars of Self-Management

The 3 pillars are:

Pillar I: Follow the core strategies of the 90-day plan as described in the previous 8 chapters.

Pillar II: Develop personal disciplines:

      i. Plan to plan,

      ii. Focus on what's important,

      iii. Judiciously defer commitment by learning not to say yes on the spot,

      iv. Step back and take the overall, fifty thousand foot view of things,

v. Learn to reflect on yourself and your reactions to situations, and

vi. Learn to know when to quit certain situations and move on.

Pillar III: Build support systems

New leaders must know how to strengthen their support systems. This will entail building a stable advice-and-counsel network, stabilize the home front, and assert control in their local environment. These will include the following:

a. Create a local infrastructure to support their work.

b. Stabilize the domestic, home front especially if moves are required by helping to acclimatize their spouses and families to new surroundings.

c. Build an advice-and-counsel network that consists of technical advisers, cultural interpreters, and political counselors.

61

Chapter 10. Accelerate Everyone

The First 90 days is a proven technique that has benefitted a multitude of organizations, which has encouraged the acceleration of any transition, regardless of what change situation it is. Whether the focus is on change implementation, performance improvement, risk management, or even all three, organizations need to accelerate transitions at every level, organizationally and individually, externally and internally.

The proper framework, systems, and tools must be put in place to accelerate everyone and improve performance. Ten design principles guidelines can guide new leaders to find and implement the appropriate solutions for their organizations:

1. Identify the Critical Transitions

2. Identify Set-Up-to-Fail Dynamics

3. Diagnose Existing Transition Support

4. Adopt a Common Core Model

5. Deliver Support Just In Time

6. Use Structured Processes

7.Match Support to Transition Type

8.Match Support to Leader Level

9. Clarify Roles and Align Incentives

10. Integrate with Other Talent Management Systems

Conclusion

A key benchmark for newly elected United States Presidents is how and what they deliver in the first one hundred days in office. The world watches if POTUS will blow up some tiny country, pass a new tax bill, or just do very little, and stay in the background until the frenzy over what the First One Hundred Days blow over. The stakes nationally and internationally probably aren't as high for new leaders in an organization, but their organizations still need them to deliver in this short transition period. The author thinks that 100 days is a little too long, and second, and that new leaders do not have the luxury of just staying in the background. Leaders cannot sit back and "chill" because, in a complex organization, things just don't "blow over."

Organizations in change situations face two types of problems. The first type is "hard" problems. There are the problems that are well structured or well defined, which can be routinely solved by the application of a well-understood formula, process or design. The tougher changes addressed in *The First 90 Days* are the so-called "soft changes," which, in change management terminology, means addressing issues that are not evident, poorly understood, dynamic, and involves the often unknowable personal agenda and feelings of everyone from the boss to the lowest clerical level type. Getting on top of the soft changes makes solving and implementing the "hard changes" much easier. Change management is even sometimes used interchangeably with soft changes and requires competent leadership.

Leadership has many perks and advantages, but especially in large and complex organizations, leaders must hit the ground running, command respect and attention from everyone in the organization, and put a recognizable individual stamp that effectively creates a "brand" for them. For many, there is at least a moment or two when newly-minted leaders not only wonder how they can navigate their way through their new roles, but may even doubt if the people who put them at the top made the right decision in the first place.

It can be a solitary journey, which is the wrong approach, even if usually just ONE leader is needed as a figurehead at the helm leading the charge. While it can be lonely at the top, going it alone is not the hallmark of a great leader, as shown by the coverage of topics in Watkin's book. At least 70% of the book, including the exercises and examples, covers how a new leader interacts with other people in the organization at all levels in and out of the organization. Chapter 4, "Negotiate Success," for example, the second longest chapter regarding pages, is practically entirely devoted on how to dealing with a new boss. Every chapter includes principles that stress the importance of garnering support and guidance from people OUTSIDE the organization.

The 90-day framework is a proven tool in many management transitions, and using it can mean the difference between an organization achieving its objectives and entirely missing the mark. Teams at every level use the same methodology, language, and tools to create 90-day plans and build relationships and teamwork. A proven acceleration system is an essential element of the organizational change management toolkit.

The First 90 Days helps new leaders assemble that toolkit.

FREE BONUSES

P.S. Is it okay if we overdeliver?

Here at Readtrepreneur Publishing, we believe in overdelivering way beyond our reader's expectations. Is it okay if we overdeliver?

Here's the deal, we're going to give you an extremely condensed PDF summary of the book which you've just read and much more...

What's the catch? We need to trust you... You see, we want to overdeliver and in order for us to do that, we've to trust our reader to keep this bonus a secret to themselves? Why? Because we don't want people to be getting our exclusive PDF summaries even without buying our books itself. Unethical, right?

Ok. Are you ready?

Firstly, remember that your book is code: "**READ96**".

Next, visit this link: http://bit.ly/exclusivepdfs

Everything else will be self explanatory after you've visited: http://bit.ly/exclusivepdfs.

We hope you'll enjoy our free bonuses as much as we enjoyed preparing it for you!

CPSIA information can be obtained
at www.ICGtesting.com
Printed in the USA
LVHW052154020819
626403LV00001B/10

9 781646 151950